WINTER OLYMPIC S[...]

FIGURE SKATING

796.912
GUS

by Joseph Gustaitis

Words that are defined in the glossary are in **bold** type the first time they appear in the text.

A table of abbreviations used for the names of countries appears on page 32.

Crabtree editor: Adrianna Morganelli
Proofreader: Crystal Sikkens
Editorial director: Kathy Middleton
Production coordinator and
   prepress technician: Katherine Berti
Developed for Crabtree Publishing Company by
RJF Publishing LLC (www.RJFpublishing.com)
Editor: Jacqueline Laks Gorman
Designer: Tammy West, Westgraphix LLC
Photo Researcher: Edward A. Thomas
Indexer: Nila Glikin

Photo Credits:
Associated Press: Wide World Photos: p. 14
Corbis: Bettmann: p. 9, 26, 27; Dimitri Iundt/TempSport: p. 13;
   Todd Korol/Reuters: p. 28
Getty Images: p. 8, 18, 24; AFP: p. 2, 4, 10, 12; Sports
   Illustrated: p. 6, 7, 16, 17, 21; Bob Thomas: p. 15, 22
Landov: Savintsev Fyodor/ITAR-TASS: p. 20; David
   Gray/Reuters: front cover
Wikipedia: Arnold C (Buchanan-Hermit): p. 29

Cover: Russia's Irina Slutskaya performs during her free skating program at the 2006 Winter Olympics.

CONTENTS

Library and Archives Canada Cataloguing in Publication

Gustaitis, Joseph Alan, 1944-
    Figure skating / Joseph Gustaitis.

(Winter Olympic sports)
Includes index.
ISBN 978-0-7787-4022-3 (bound).--ISBN 978-0-7787-4041-4 (pbk.)

    1. Figure skating--Juvenile literature. 2. Winter Olympics--Juvenile literature. I. Title. II. Series: Winter Olympic sports

GV850.4.G88 2009   j796.91'2   C2009-903212-0

Library of Congress Cataloging-in-Publication Data

Gustaitis, Joseph Alan, 1944-
    Figure skating / Joseph Gustaitis.
       p. cm. -- (Winter Olympic Sports)
    ISBN 978-0-7787-4022-3 (reinforced library binding : alk. paper)
 -- ISBN 978-0-7787-4041-4 (pbk. : alk. paper)
    1. Figure skating--I. Title. II. Series.

GV850.4.G87 2009
796.91'2--dc22   2009021492

Crabtree Publishing Company

Published in Canada
Crabtree Publishing
616 Welland Ave.
St. Catharines, ON
L2M 5V6

Published in the United States
Crabtree Publishing
PMB16A
350 Fifth Ave., Suite 3308
New York, NY 10118

Published in the United Kingdom
Crabtree Publishing
White Cross Mills
High Town, Lancaster
LA1 4XS

Published in Australia
Crabtree Publishing
386 Mt. Alexander Rd.
Ascot Vale (Melbourne)
VIC 3032

FROM THE BEGINNING

Ice skates were not invented for fun, but for transportation. Today, figure skating is one of the most entertaining events in the Olympic Games!

THE FIRST SUPERSTAR

The first skating star was Jackson Haines (USA), who was born in 1840. At the time, figure skating was rather formal and movements were not flowing. Haines developed a new style of skating that was more graceful and dramatic. When he went to Europe to skate, he shocked everyone by skating to music!

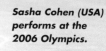

Sasha Cohen (USA) performs at the 2006 Olympics.

DID YOU KNOW?

Figure skating was included in the Olympics in 1908 and 1920, but they were Summer Olympics!

ANCIENT ORIGINS

About 3,000 years ago, people in northern Europe invented skates to get across frozen lakes. The blades were made from animal bones. Iron blades were invented about 1,000 years later.

MODERN ICE SKATING

The sport of figure skating started in England in the 1800s, then it came to North America. Around the year 1850, a man named E. V. Bushnell invented a special steel skate that let skaters jump and **spin** in exciting ways.

FIRST WINTER WINNERS

At the first Winter Olympic Games in 1924, Gillis Grafström (SWE) won the men's gold medal in figure skating. Herma Planck-Szabo (AUT) won the women's competition. The winners in pairs were Helene Engelmann and Alfred Berger (AUT). There was no ice dance competition at the time.

- The Olympic Games were first held in Olympia, in ancient Greece, around 3,000 years ago. They took place every four years until they were abolished in 393 A.D. A Frenchman named Pierre Coubertin (1863–1937) revived the Games, and the first modern Olympics—which featured only summer sports—were held in Athens in 1896.

- The first Olympic Winter Games were held in 1924 in Chamonix, France. The Winter Games were then held every four years except in 1940 and 1944 (because of World War II), taking place in the same year as the Summer Games, until 1992.

- The International Olympic Committee decided to stage the Summer and Winter Games in different years, so there was only a two-year gap before the next Winter Games were held in 1994. They have been held every four years from that time.

- The symbol of the Olympic Games is five interlocking colored rings. Together, they represent the union of the five regions of the world—Africa, the Americas, Asia, Europe, and Oceania (Australia and the Pacific Islands)—as athletes come together to compete in the Games.

JUMPS AND OTHER MOVES

Jumps are the most exciting moves in figure skating. The best jumper often wins the competition. There are two basic kinds of jumps—**edge jumps** and **toe jumps**. Jumps can be done in combination, one after another.

NOT JUST JUMPS

A figure skating program involves more than just jumps. Other important elements are spins, **spirals**, and steps that connect the parts of the program together. These moves also show the skater's grace, flexibility, and skill.

Alexei Yagudin (RUS) executes one of the jumps that helped him win the 2002 Olympics.

ON THE EDGE

In edge jumps, the skater takes off from an edge of the skate. The three most common are the **Axel**, **Salchow**, and **loop**. The Axel is special because it's the only jump a skater does going forward. The skater winds up facing backward, so the Axel has an extra half turn in the air.

FROM THE TOE

In a toe jump, the skater uses the toe pick of one skate on takeoff. This helps the skater jump higher. Toe jumps include the **toe loop**, **flip**, and **Lutz**.

DOUBLES AND TRIPLES

If a skater spins once in the air after taking off, he's done a single jump. If he spins twice, it's a double jump, and if he spins three times, it's a triple jump. The triple Axel is 3 1/2 turns in the air. The first man to do one in competition was Vern Taylor (CAN) in 1978. Midori Ito (JPN) was the first woman to do one in competition, in 1989.

QUADS

A quad is a **quadruple** jump—four turns in the air! Kurt Browning (CAN) was the first skater to do a quad in competition, at the 1988 World Championships. Petr Barna (CZE) did the first quad in the Olympics in 1992.

IMPROPER BEHAVIOR?

Theresa Weld (USA) performed the first jump ever done by a woman in competition—a single Salchow, done at the 1920 Olympics. The judges scolded her for being "unladylike."

DID YOU KNOW?

Brian Orser (CAN) did the first triple Axel in the Olympics in 1984. Eight years later, Midori Ito (JPN) became the first woman to do the jump at the Olympics.

WHAT'S IN A NAME?

Some skating moves are named after the skaters who invented them or made them popular. One famous move is the Biellmann spin—named after Denise Biellmann (SUI)—in which the skater arches her back and holds one leg high above her head. (Men can do Biellmann spins if they're very flexible, but most of them aren't able to.)

OOPS!

Skaters can make mistakes when they jump. Some of the mistakes have special names. A "cheat" means the skater didn't fully turn in the air—for example, turning only two times instead of three when trying to perform a triple jump. A "waxel" is a failed attempt at an Axel jump. A "flutz" was supposed to be a Lutz jump, but the skater took off the wrong way, as if he was doing a flip jump instead of a Lutz.

THE OLYMPIC EVENTS

Women's singles, men's singles, pairs, and ice dance are the four figure skating events featured at the Olympics.

Scott Hamilton (USA) celebrates at the 1984 Winter Games.

SINGLES COMPETITION

The women's and men's competitions have two parts — the **short program** and the **free skating program** (or long program). Both are done to music. The short program lasts a maximum of two minutes and 50 seconds. A skater has to do eight required elements, such as jumps and spins. The free skate is four minutes long for women and 4 1/2 minutes long for men. It doesn't have all the required parts that the short program has.

A maximum of 30 women and 30 men participate in the Olympics in figure skating. The 24 women and men who do the best in the short program advance to the free program. A maximum of 20 pairs and 24 ice dance couples also participate. All of them advance to the last part of the competition.

DID YOU KNOW?

Athletes from Russia or the Soviet Union have won the most medals in Olympic figure skating, with 49. The United States is next, with 44.

PAIRS

Pairs skating is done by two skaters together. Each pair does a short program with required parts and a free skating program. The two skaters perform the same jumps and spins that singles skaters do, but they do them at the same time. Pairs also do special moves like **throw jumps** and overhead **lifts**.

ICE DANCE

Ice dance, which is done by two people, is like ballroom dancing on ice. The footwork is very difficult. Ice dance has three parts—the compulsory dance, the original dance, and the free dance.

THE OLYMPIC RINK

In the 2010 Olympics in Vancouver, figure skating will take place at the Pacific Coliseum. The rink is 197 feet (60 meters) long and 98 feet (30 meters) wide.

BOOTS AND BLADES

Top figure skaters wear expensive skate boots that have been custom-made for them. The boots have thick, stiff leather interiors and added support around the ankles. The tongues have padding for flexibility. The blades, which have a slight curve, are specially sharpened. The width of the blade is about 0.15 inches to 0.25 inches (0.38 cm to 0.63 cm).

A spin by Midori Ito (JPN) at the 1992 Games.

THE WOMEN

The women's singles is the most popular figure skating event at any Winter Olympics.

A FIRST FOR JAPAN

When Shizuka Arakawa (JPN) won the gold medal at the 2006 Olympics, she became the first Japanese figure skater to win Olympic gold. Arakawa had to come back from third place in the short program!

Beautiful moves helped Shizuka Arakawa (JPN) win the gold in 2006.

2006 OLYMPIC MEDALISTS: GOLD: SHIZUKA ARAKAWA (JPN)

SUPER STATS

The United States has won the gold medal in women's figure skating a record seven times.

DID YOU KNOW?

Women figure skaters used to wear heavy clothing and long skirts. Sonja Henie (NOR) was the first to wear knee-length skirts. Some judges did not like that.

THREE-PEAT

Sonja Henie (NOR) may have been the greatest woman figure skater ever. She is the only woman to win three Olympic gold medals in figure skating (1928, 1932, 1936). She also won ten World Championships! After the Olympics, she became a movie star.

FROM LAST TO FIRST

Sonja Henie (NOR) first appeared at the Olympics in 1924, when she was only 11 years old. She came in last! At the next Olympics, she rose to the top and came in first.

YOUNGEST AND OLDEST

The oldest woman to win an Olympic gold medal in figure skating was also the first—Madge Syers (GBR). She won in 1908 at the age of 27. In 1998, Tara Lipinski (USA) became the youngest winner. She was only 15! She is also the youngest person to win an individual event in Winter Olympic history.

LET'S DANCE

Many Olympic champions skate in ice shows after the Olympics. Kristi Yamaguchi (USA), the 1992 champion, starred in the Stars on Ice show. In 2008, she went on the TV show *Dancing With the Stars* and won first prize.

A LONG CAREER

Irina Slutskaya (RUS), the bronze medal winner at the 2006 Olympics, had a long and brilliant career. She competed at the World Championships for the first time in 1995 and won six medals—including two golds—over the next few years. She also won a silver medal at the 2002 Olympics. She retired from competition after 2006.

Sonja Henie (NOR), winner of three Olympic championships.

GREAT MOMENTS IN WOMEN'S FIGURE SKATING

Great performances, beautiful costumes, and upsets—that's why people watch women's figure skating!

Katarina Witt (GDR), in the performance that won her a second Olympic gold medal in 1988.

DUELING CARMENS

A funny thing happened in 1988—two skaters chose the same music. They were Katarina Witt (GDR), who had won in 1984, and Debi Thomas (USA). The music was from the opera *Carmen*. Witt won the Olympic gold medal. Elizabeth Manley (CAN) finished second, and Thomas finished third.

COMEBACK

When Tenley Albright (USA) was 11, she came down with a case of polio, a serious disease that affects the muscles. She recovered and went on to become a top skater. She almost didn't win the Olympics in 1956, though. Two weeks before the Games, she hit a rut on the ice while practicing, and one of her skates cut through the other, slashing a blood vessel in her leg. Albright's father—a doctor—fixed her up, and she was off to the Olympics! There, she won the first-place votes of 10 of the 11 judges.

HARDING AND KERRIGAN

The showdown between two U.S. skaters at the 1994 Winter Olympics was one of the most watched TV shows ever. A month before the Olympics, an attacker clubbed Nancy Kerrigan on the knee. The ex-husband of skater Tonya Harding had hired the man so Kerrigan would not be able to skate in the Olympics. Kerrigan recovered in time and won the silver medal behind Oksana Baiul (UKR). Harding finished eighth.

THE BIG UPSET

Few people thought Sarah Hughes (USA) would win the gold medal in 2002. The favorite was Michelle Kwan (USA), who was the World Champion. Things looked bad for Hughes going into the free skate. She was in fourth place, but she skated the best performance of her life and won the gold medal. Kwan wound up third. Kwan was one of the most popular figure skaters ever, but she never won an Olympic gold medal.

CLOSE COMPETITION

The 1980 Olympics featured one of the closest competitions ever in the women's event. Annett Pötzsch (GDR) and Linda Fratienne (USA) had both been World Champions in the years leading up to the Olympics. Both skated well at the Games, with Pötzsch winning the **figures** while Fratienne won the short program. In the end, Pötzsch skated away with the gold. Fratienne settled for silver.

THE MEN

In every Olympics, the men's singles competition keeps getting better, as the skaters perform fantastic feats.

A spectacular move by Evgeni Plushenko (RUS), the winner of the gold medal in 2006.

COMBO KING

Evgeni Plushenko (RUS) does amazing combinations of jumps. He was the first to do a "4–3–3" during a competition. In a 4–3–3, the skater does a quadruple jump, then two triple jumps — without stopping in between. No wonder Plushenko won the gold medal at the 2006 Olympics!

THREE-TIME WINNER

Only one man has won the Olympic gold medal in figure skating three times — Gillis Grafström (SWE). He won in 1920, 1924, and 1928, then he won silver in 1932. Grafström is also the only skater to win medals in four Olympics.

SUPER STATS

Male skaters from Russia or the Soviet Union have won the gold medal in every Olympics since 1992.

DID YOU KNOW?

When Ilia Kulik (RUS) won Olympic gold in 1998, it was the first time he was in the Olympics. The last man to do that was Dick Button (USA) in 1948.

THE BALLET DANCER

When John Curry (GBR) was young, he wanted to be a ballet dancer. His father wanted him to go into sports, and Curry chose skating. Curry combined great jumps with great art. He won the gold medal in 1976.

STILL FAMOUS

It has been more than 50 years since Dick Button (USA) won his second gold medal, but he might still be the most famous male figure skater. Button was not afraid to try really hard jumps during a competition. He was the first skater to do a double Axel (when he won in 1948) and a triple jump (when he won in 1952). After that, he became a TV announcer.

YOU CAN'T DO THAT AGAIN

Terry Kubicka (USA) did the only legal back flip ever in Olympic history in 1976. After the Games, the move was ruled illegal. Skating officials said that since the back flip is landed on two feet instead of one, it's not a "real" jump. The back flip may also be considered too dangerous. Kubicka came in seventh, and the back flip became a popular move in skating shows.

Elvis Stojko, one of Canada's finest, won two silver medals in the Olympics.

GREAT MOMENTS IN MEN'S FIGURE SKATING

Some of the most exciting athletes in Olympic history have been male figure skaters.

THE BATTLE OF THE BRIANS

Brian Boitano (USA) and Brian Orser (CAN) will always be connected. They skated against each other for years. One would win, and then the other. Everybody was excited when they met in the Olympics in 1988. In the free skate, Boitano skated first and delivered one of the best performances in Olympic history. Orser did almost as well, but he made a few little mistakes. Boitano won gold, and Orser won silver.

RUNNERS-UP

No Canadian man has ever won the Olympic figure skating championship, but some have come close. Brian Orser won silver medals in 1984 and 1988. Elvis Stojko won silver medals in 1994 and 1998. Stojko was a great jumper who studied martial arts. He was the favorite in 1998, but he had a painful injury and could not do his best jumps.

OH, BROTHER!

In 1956, Hayes Alan Jenkins (USA) won the gold medal and his brother, David, won bronze. Four years later, David won the gold, too!

FAST LEARNER

Evgeni Plushenko (RUS), the 2006 winner, could do all the triple jumps by the time he was 11 years old.

BEATING THE ODDS

Scott Hamilton (USA), the 1984 champion, is one of the world's most popular skaters. When he was a little boy, he had a disease that stopped him from growing. He wound up being only about 5'3" (1.6 m) tall.

Brian Orser (CAN) won silver medals in 1984 and 1988.

YOU MUST REMEMBER THIS

Sometimes a figure skater gives a special performance but doesn't win a medal. That's what happened at the 1994 Games to Kurt Browning (CAN). Browning was way behind in the standings after falling in the short program. In his free skate, he dressed up like the character played by actor Humphrey Bogart in the classic movie *Casablanca*. He also skated to music from the movie. Browning finished fifth, but he changed figure skating by adding a special dose of show business.

QUADS ALL OVER

The 2002 Olympics featured some of the most amazing skating ever in the men's long program. The three men's medalists — Alexei Yagudin (RUS), Evgeni Plushenko (RUS), and Timothy Goebel (USA) — each did two quadruple jumps in the free program!

THE PAIRS

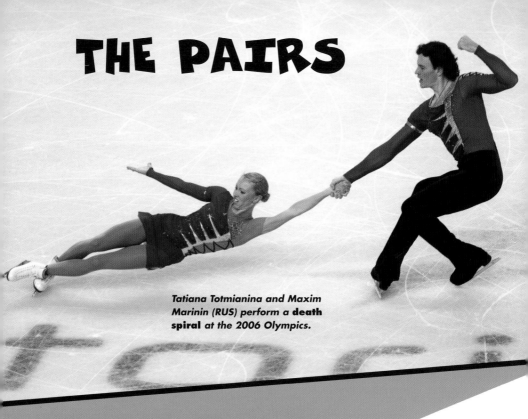

Tatiana Totmianina and Maxim Marinin (RUS) perform a **death spiral** at the 2006 Olympics.

Pairs skaters—a man and a woman on the ice side by side—must perform difficult moves together with perfect timing and skill.

LEARN THE LINGO

Here are some pairs skating moves:

Spins—Skaters do some spins side by side. They also do "pair spins," where they hold each other.

Lifts—During a lift, the man holds the woman in the air. Sometimes she changes position during the lift.

Throw jumps—In a throw jump, the man launches the woman into one of the jumps that are done in singles skating.

Death spiral—In this scary-sounding move, the man turns while holding the woman's hand. She stretches out, almost lying on the ice, and goes in a circle around him.

OOPS!

Pairs skating can be dangerous. The woman can fall during a lift. In 2004, Tatiana Totmianina and Maxim Marinin (RUS) were skating in Pittsburgh. He lifted her into the air, but he tripped and she fell. She crashed onto the ice and had to go to the hospital. The pair did not compete for a while, but they came back to win the Olympics in 2006!

Zhang Dan and Zhang Hao (CHN) in action in 2006.

CHANGING PARTNERS

Pairs skaters don't always stay with the same partner. Irina Rodnina (URS) won the gold medal in 1972 skating with Aleksey Ulanov. Ulanov fell in love with a different skater, so Rodnina came to the 1976 Olympics with a new partner—her new husband, Aleksandr Zaytsev. They won in both 1976 and 1980.

IN THE MIRROR

A man and woman in a pair usually jump and spin in the same direction, either to the left or to the right. Sometimes, though, the two people in a pair jump and spin in opposite directions. This is called mirror skating. One successful pair who did mirror skating were Jill Watson and Peter Oppegard (USA), who won the bronze medal in 1988.

SPECTACULAR FALL

During the free skate at the 2006 Olympics, Zhang Dan and Zhang Hao (CHN) attempted a very difficult move—a throw quadruple Salchow, which no pair had ever done successfully in competition before. She fell, though, and hurt her knee badly. The music stopped, and officials made sure she could skate. After a delay, the pair was able to continue. The crowd stood and applauded when they were done. Zhang and Zhang won the silver medal.

PAIRS: JUDGES, JUMPS, AND ROMANCE

Pairs have been involved in some of the most dramatic moments in Olympic figure skating.

Both the Russian and Canadian pairs were awarded gold medals in 2002.

THE GREAT JUDGING SCANDAL

After the short program at the 2002 Olympics, Elena Berezhnaya and Anton Sikharulidze (RUS) were in first place. Jamie Salé and David Pelletier (CAN) were in second. Both teams skated well in the free skate, but the Russians made one small mistake. The Canadians were perfect. Many people thought they had won, but the judges gave the gold medal to the Russians. Later, one of the judges said she had been "pressured" to vote for the Russians. Olympic officials decided to give a second gold medal to Salé and Pelletier.

ROMANCE ON ICE

Sometimes pairs skaters fall in love and get married. Ludovika and Walter Jakobsson (FIN) were the first husband and wife team to win a gold medal, in 1920. Andrée and Pierre Brunet (FRA) won the gold medal twice, in 1928 and 1932. So did another married couple, Lyudmilla Belousova and Oleg Protopopov (URS), in 1964 and 1968.

THE SADDEST THING

Ekaterina Gordeeva and Sergei Grinkov (URS) won the gold medal in 1988. Three years later, they got married. In 1994, they won the gold medal again. But in 1995, Grinkov had a heart attack and died. It was one of the saddest things that ever happened in figure skating.

TURNING OVER A NEW LEAF

Artur Dmitriev and Natalia Mishkutenok (RUS) won the gold medal in pairs at the 1992 Olympics, then the silver medal in 1994. She decided to retire, but he wanted to continue skating. He found a new partner, Oksana Kazakova, and they won the gold medal in 1998. He became the first man ever to win the pairs competition at the Olympics with different partners.

FAMILY TIES

Sometimes pairs skaters are brother and sister. Kitty and Peter Carruthers (USA) were adopted when they were little children. At the 1984 Olympics, they won the silver medal.

TOO BAD

In 1980, skating fans were looking forward to a great Olympic contest, but it never happened. Irina Rodnina and Aleksandr Zaytsev (URS) were World Champions from 1973 to 1978. They took a year off in 1979 when Rodnina had a baby. That year, Tai Babilonia and Randy Gardner (USA) became World Champions. Which pair would win the Olympics in 1980? Unfortunately, Gardner got hurt, and he and Babilonia had to pull out of the competition.

ICE DANCE

A marvelous move by ice dancers Tatiana Navka and Roman Kostomarov (RUS).

Ice dance is somewhat like pairs skating, since a man and woman skate together to music. But in many ways, ice dance is very different.

A BRIEF HISTORY

Ice dance began in the last half of the 1800s. After skater Jackson Haines went to Europe, ice dance began to catch on. It was very popular in Vienna, Austria. There, dancers did the waltz on ice. Soon, waltzing on ice was popular in other countries. Other dances were also done on the ice. A book published in 1892 showed 17 different ice dances!

LEARN THE LINGO

Here are the three parts of ice dance competition:

Compulsory dance — All the couples do the same steps to a specific type of music.

Original dance — The skaters can choose the music, but everyone's music must be to a particular rhythm.

Free dance — This part has the fewest rules. The skaters can choose the music and the theme and can use unusual and difficult positions.

A LOT OF DANCES

The **International Skating Union** (ISU) announces what compulsory dances couples will do each year. Ice dancers have to learn a lot of dances! Some of them are the Argentine Tango, Blues, Cha Cha Congelado, Foxtrot, Paso Doble, and Yankee Polka.

GETTING DIZZY

Twizzles — turns done on one foot — are required moves in ice dance programs. Skaters usually do at least four turns during a twizzle.

Tanith Belbin and Benjamin Agosto gave the United States its first medal in ice dance in 30 years.

WHAT'S DIFFERENT ABOUT DANCE?

Ice dance doesn't have jumps. Lifts are done, but rules carefully spell out how high the woman can be raised. The skaters must also be close together and hold each other for much of the program. Lyrics are allowed in ice dance music — but not for other types of figure skating!

THE GREAT DANCERS

The magnificent Jayne Torvill and Christopher Dean (GBR) during the 1984 Olympics.

It takes a special twosome of skaters to win an ice dance competition. The Olympics have seen quite a few.

DID YOU KNOW?

Tatiana Navka (RUS), who won the gold in ice dance in 2006 with her partner, Roman Kostomarov, is married to Aleksandr Zhulin, who won Olympic medals in 1992 and 1994 with his partner, Maia Usova. Zhulin is also Navka's coach!

THE FIRST OLYMPIC COMPETITION

When ice dance first appeared in the Olympics in 1976, Lyudmila Pakhomova and Aleksandr Gorshkov (URS) won the first gold medal. It was only a year after Gorshkov had a serious lung operation. Colleen O'Connor and Jim Millins (USA) won the bronze medal. The United States did not win another Olympic medal in ice dance for 30 years, until Tanith Belbin and Benjamin Agosto took silver in 2006.

THE BEST

Most people think that the best ice dance team ever was Jayne Torvill and Christopher Dean (GBR). They created a new style that changed ice dance forever. Once, they skated to music from a Broadway show and acted out the characters. Sometimes they used rock and roll, and other times they used Spanish music. After their free dance at the 1984 Olympics, the judges gave them 12 perfect scores! Ten years later, they returned to the Olympics and finished third. He was 35 years old, and she was 36.

TWO-TIME WINNERS

Only one couple has won the Olympic gold medal in ice dance twice—Oksana Grishuk and Evgeny Platov (RUS). They won in 1994 and 1998. One of the teams they beat in 1994 was Torvill and Dean.

GOLD AT LAST

Marina Klimova and Sergei Ponomarenko (URS) worked their way up the ranks. They won a bronze medal in 1984, a silver medal in 1988, and finally a gold medal in 1992. They are the only figure skaters to win three medals of different colors in the Olympics. They also won eight World Championship medals, including three golds.

CHEERS AND BOOS

The crowd was not happy with the results of the ice dance competition at the 1980 Winter Olympics. The gold medal winners, Natalia Linichuk and Gennadi Karponossov (URS), were formal, traditional ice dancers. The audience preferred the silver medal winners, Krisztina Regöczy and Andras Sallay (HUN), who skated in a more lively, upbeat style.

JUDGING

In many sports, it's easy to see who's the best. It's the person who swims fastest or jumps highest. But how do you know who's the best in figure skating?

The judges watching Jeffrey Buttle (CAN) at the 2006 Games.

WAITING FOR THE SCORES

At competitions, skaters and their coaches wait for the scores to be announced in an area near the ice called the "Kiss and Cry." That's because they'll be happy if the scores are good but sad if the scores are bad.

FIGURE SKATING JUDGES

The panel of judges who score each figure skating program have a difficult job, since it's hard to vote against a skater from your own country. The ISU makes the rules for judging international competitions. After the judging trouble at the 2002 Olympics, when one judge said she was pressured to vote a certain way, the ISU decided to set up a new judging system.

THE OLD SYSTEM

In the old system, each judge gave two marks. The first—for technical merit—judged things like how difficult the jumps were. The second mark—for presentation—judged the skater's style and how well she performed. Judges gave marks up to 6.0. A mark of 6.0 was "perfect."

THE NEW SYSTEM

The new judging system is much more complicated. Judges give two marks. The first mark—for technical elements—refers to the different moves a skater does. Every jump and every spin has a value assigned to it. Points are also added or taken away for how well or how poorly a move was done. The second mark—for program components—refers to the overall presentation of the program. The marks are added up for the skater's total score.

DIFFERENT MARKS FOR DIFFERENT MOVES

The harder the move, the more it's worth. A triple Axel has a base value of 8.2 points, while a double Axel is worth only 3.5 points. A triple Lutz has a base value of 6 points. Quadruple jumps are worth much more. A quadruple top loop has a base value of 9.8 points, and a quadruple Salchow has a value of 10.3 points. Some skaters think that quads are so hard that they should be worth even more!

WHAT ARE FIGURES?

Did you ever wonder why figure skating is called "figure" skating?

Janet Lynn (USA) did not win the Olympics because she did poorly in figures.

FIGURES AT THE OLYMPICS

Doing figures was a major part of early Olympic competition. In fact, at the first Olympic figure skating competition in 1908, "Special Figures" was a separate event. The gold medal winner was Nicolai Panin (RUS).

FANCY PATTERNS

Long ago, skaters saw that their sharp skate blades could cut lines into the ice. At first, they did simple patterns like a circle or a figure 8. Then they learned to do harder patterns. These patterns were called figures. Figures had fancy names like "the flying Mercury" and "the shamrock."

THE END OF FIGURES

Scott Hamilton (USA) tracing a figure.

In the early 1970s, figures were worth 60% of a skater's total score. The free skate was worth only 40%. The ISU decided to lower the value of figures and add the short program, beginning with the 1976 Olympics. Eventually, the figures were dropped entirely. The first Olympics without figures were in 1992.

DID YOU KNOW?

Skaters used to spend hours every day working on their figures. This helped them learn body control and patience, but took time away from practicing jumps. Many skaters were happy when the figures were eliminated from the competition.

BECAUSE OF FIGURES ...

Sometimes a great skater did not win a gold medal because of the figures. In the 1970s, Janet Lynn (USA) was one of the best and most popular skaters in the world. But at the 1972 Olympics, Trixi Schuba (AUT) was so good at figures that she won the gold. Lynn won the free program but wound up with the bronze.

EXAMINING THE ICE

After a competitor finished skating a figure, the judges would come out on the ice to examine the tracing. They would look closely at the figure, even getting down on their hands and knees to get a really close view. They looked to see if the circles were perfectly round and if all the circles were the same size. They also checked to make sure the skating edges were smooth.

CUTTING THE ICE

Jeannette Altwegg (GBR), who won the gold medal in 1952, was famous for her figures. When she skated one particular figure, she skated two circles, one on top of the other. A reporter said that it looked like she had "cut the ice only once."

A SNAPSHOT OF THE VANCOUVER 2010 WINTER OLYMPICS

FIGURE SKATING
THE ATHLETES

Everyone is getting ready for Vancouver in 2010! Olympic teams
are still being determined. The listings below include the top finishers
in a selection of events from the 2009 World Figure Skating
Championships. Who among them will be the athletes to watch in the
Vancouver Winter Olympics? Visit the Web site www.vancouver2010.com
for more information about the upcoming competitions.

FIGURE SKATING EVENTS

Men — free skate:
1. Evan Lysacek (USA)
2. Patrick Chan (CAN)
3. Brian Joubert (FRA)
4. Tomas Verner (CZE)
5. Samuel Contesti (ITA)

Women — free skate:
1. Kim Yu-Na (KOR)
2. Miki Ando (JPN)
3. Joannie Rochette (CAN)
4. Mao Asada (JPN)
5. Rachel Flat (USA)

Pairs — free skate:
1. Aliona Savchenko/
   Robin Szolkowy (GER)
2. Zhang Dan/
   Zhang Hao (CHN)
3. Yuko Kavaguti/
   Alexander Smirnov
   (RUS)
4. Pang Qing/
   Tong Jian (CHN)
5. Tatiana Volosozhar/
   Stanislav Morozov (UKR)

*Evan Lysacek (USA) performs
his men's short program,
during the Torino 2006
Figure Skating competition.*

Ice dancing—original dance:
1. Tanith Belbin/Benjamin Agosto (USA)
2. Oksana Domnina/Maxim Shabalin (RUS)
3. Meryl Davis/Charlie White (USA)
4. Nathalie Pechalat/Fabian Bourzat (FRA)
5. Jana Khokhlova/Sergei Novitski (RUS)

Ice dancing—free dance:
1. Oksana Domnina/Maxim Shabalin (RUS)
2. Tanith Belbin/Benjamin Agosto (USA)
3. Meryl Davis/Charlie White (USA)
4. Tessa Virtue/Scott Moir (CAN)
5. Nathalie Pechalat/Fabian Bourzat (FRA)

Tessa Virtue and Scott Moir of Canada perform their gold medal routine in the senior dance free program at the 2009 Canadian Figure Skating Championships.

THE VENUE IN VANCOUVER
PACIFIC COLISEUM

- **venue capacity: 14,239**
- **located in Vancouver, British Columbia**
- **elevation: 85 feet (26 m)**

GLOSSARY

Axel An edge jump in which the skater takes off from the forward outside edge of one foot and lands on the back outside edge of the other foot; the only jump a skater does going forward

death spiral In pairs skating, a move in which the woman stretches out horizontal to the ice while holding the man's hand as he turns

edge jump A jump in which the skater takes off from an edge of the skate

figures Formerly a part of figure skating competitions in which skaters were required to trace certain patterns on the ice

flip A toe jump in which the skater skates backward on a back inside edge, picks with the toe of one skate, makes a turn, and lands on the back outside edge of the other foot

free skating program The second part in singles and pairs competitions; sometimes called the long program

International Skating Union The ISU, the international governing body of both figure skating and speed skating

lift In pairs skating, a move in which the man holds the woman in the air

loop An edge jump in which the skater takes off from a back outside edge, turns in the air, and lands backward on the same edge

Lutz A toe jump in which the skater takes off from a back outside edge and lands on the back outside edge of the other foot

quadruple A jump in which the skater turns four times in the air; also known as a quad

Salchow An edge jump in which the skater takes off from a back inside edge, turns, and lands on the back outside edge of the opposite foot

short program The first part of singles and pairs competitions containing certain required elements

spin A move in which the skater spins on the ice like a top

spiral A move in which the skater glides across the ice with the non-skating leg extended into the air

throw jump In pairs skating, a move in which the woman does a jump after the man throws her into the air

toe jump A jump in which the skater is assisted by using the toe pick on one skate

toe loop A toe jump in which the skater takes off and lands on the same outside edge

FIND OUT MORE

BOOKS

Browning, Kurt. *A is for Axel: An Ice Skating Alphabet* (Farmington Hills, MI: Sleeping Bear Press, 2005)

Buckley, James. *Ice Skating Stars* (New York: DK Children, 2004)

Helmer, Diana Star, and Thomas S. Owens. *The History of Figure Skating* (New York: Rosen Publishing Group, 2005)

Jones, Jen. *Figure Skating for Fun!* (Minneapolis: Compass Point Books, 2006)

Milton, Steve. *Figure Skating Today: The Next Wave of Stars* (Richmond Hill, Ontario: Firefly Books, 2007)

Samuels, Rikki. *Kids' Book of Figure Skating: Skills, Strategies, and Techniques* (New York: Citadel Press Books, 2004)

Schwartz, Heather E. *Girls' Figure Skating: Ruling the Rink* (Mankato, MN: Capstone Press, 2007)

Thomas, Keltie. *How Figure Skating Works* (Toronto: Maple Tree Press, 2009)

WEB SITES

Skate Canada   www.skatecanada.ca
The Web site of Skate Canada, the national governing body of figure skating in Canada.

Canadian Olympic Committee   www.olympic.ca
The official site of the Canadian Olympic Committee, with information on athletes, sports, and the Olympics.

Golden Skate   www.goldenskate.com
A site that has news, articles, competition results, and other information about figure skating.

International Olympic Committee   www.olympic.org
The official site of the International Olympic Committee, with information on all Olympic sports.

International Skating Union   www.isu.org
The official site of the world governing body of skating.

Skateweb   www.frogsonice.com/skateweb
A Web site with links to all sorts of information about figure skating.

U.S. Figure Skating   www.usfigureskating.org
The Web site of U.S. Figure Skating, the national governing body of figure skating in the United States.

U.S. Olympic Committee   www.usoc.org/
The official site of the U.S. Olympic Committee, with information on athletes, sports, and the Olympics.

INDEX

COUNTRY ABBREVIATIONS

AUT — Austria

CAN — Canada

CHN — China

CZE — Czechoslovakia/Czech Republic

FIN — Finland

FRA — France

GBR — Great Britain

GDR — East Germany (1949–1990)

HUN — Hungary

JPN — Japan

NOR — Norway

RUS — Russia

SUI — Switzerland

SWE — Sweden

UKR — Ukraine

URS — Soviet Union (1922–1992)

USA — United States of America

Printed in the U.S.A. — CG